Swiss Shorthaired F
20 Milestone Chal

Swiss Shorthaired Pinscher Memorable Moments.
Includes Milestones for Memories, Gifts, Socialization & Training

Volume 1

Todays Doggy

Dedicated To All of You Wonderful Owners and Fans

Introduction

Welcome to the Original Doggy Milestone Series™ where you are encouraged to create those special moments with your dog. We have composed the milestones in a way that challenges you to set the stage before taking your photos.

Use props and make it fun - be creative in setting up your photos. Get family and friends involved - take it out with you - use it in different places and settings - have a play with it and most importantly, have a good time!

You can either hold the desired milestone spread open yourself - or have somebody hold it open as you take the snap.

If you would like to have the selected milestone book spread open and standing independently in your photos, you can use one or two large 'foldback' clips to hold the spread open.

Good luck and enjoy your photo fun.

I Love My Family...

...And My Family Loves Me

At The
Beach!

Having
a
Wave
of a
Time

NIGHT OUT

With My Doggy Pals

IT'S...

BED TIME

I DIDN'T KNOW WHICH STICK YOU THREW

SO I BOUGHT BACK ALL OF THEM

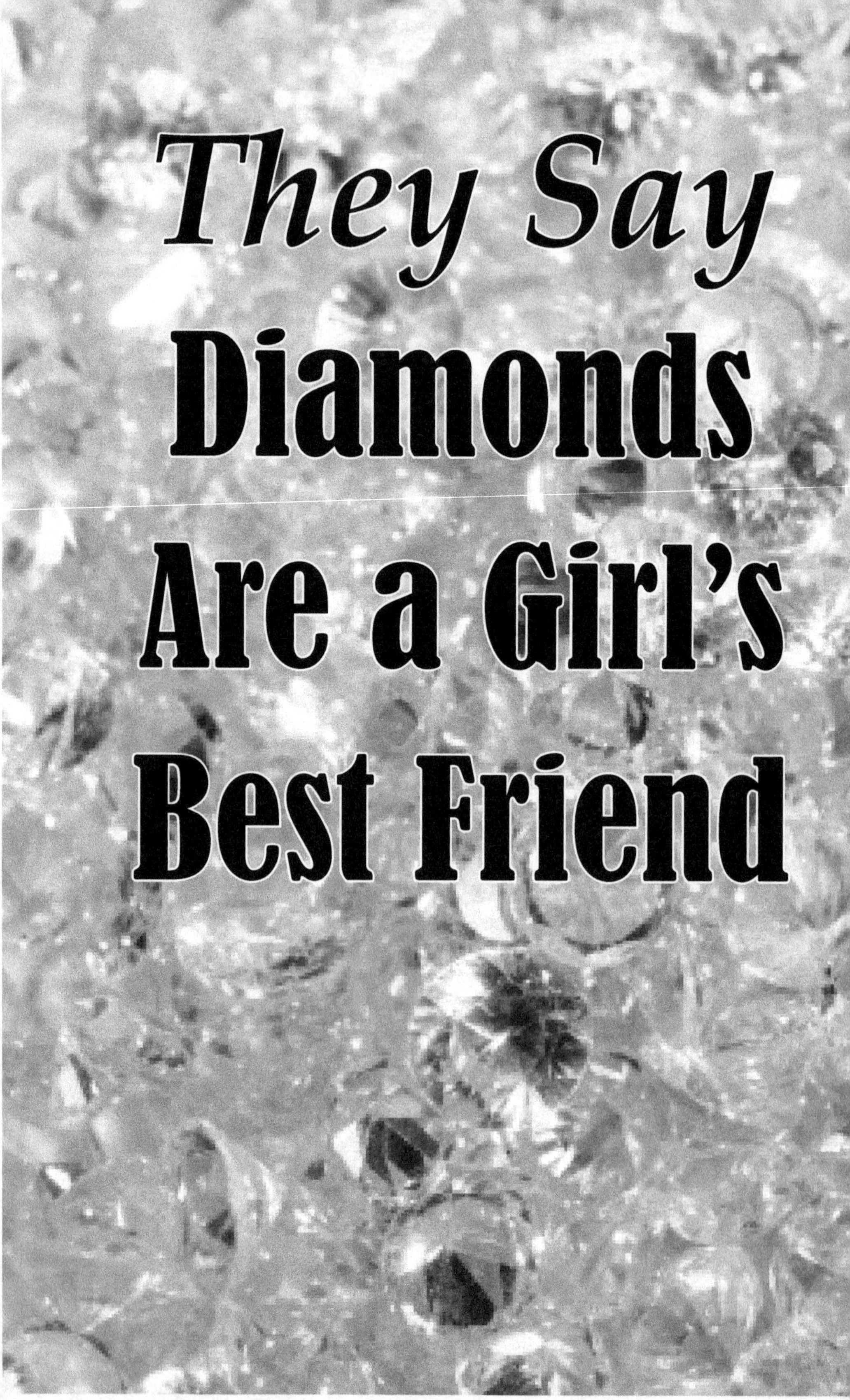
They Say
Diamonds
Are a Girl's
Best Friend

I Disagree! I'm The Only "*Best Friend*" Here!

I'm Going To Start Eating Healthy...

Next Week!

DO
NOT
DISTURB

PLAYING IN THE LEAVES

I Need

a

HUGe

Amount of Treats

Say

ello

To My Little Friend

OFF

To

The

VET??

CATCH ME IF YOU CAN!

KEEP
CALM

WE'RE
A
TEAM

NASA Wants To Hire Me

Because I'm a STAR!

OOPS! I Buried Your Stuff

...But I Forgot Where

I’m a Super Hero

My Real Name Is SUPER POOCH

VIP

Very Incredible Pup

I

DIDN'T

DO IT

I'll Just Be Over Here...

Looking Fabulous

PLEASE

PLEASE

PRETTY PLEEEASE

CAN I KEEP IT?

I'm On a SEAFOOD Diet

When I SEE FOOD, I EAT IT!

CPSIA information can be obtained
at www.ICGtesting.com
Printed in the USA
LVHW080321200819
628164LV00012B/2365/P

9 781395 334185